WHAT GOOD THING HAPPENED TO YOU TODAY?

Coloured by: _____

Written by: **VALERIE J KULCHISKY**

Illustrated by: **Stephen Armstrong**

BALBOA.PRESS

A DIVISION OF HAY HOUSE

Balboa Press books may be ordered through booksellers or by contacting:

Balboa Press
A Division of Hay House
1663 Liberty Drive
Bloomington, IN 47403
www.balboapress.com
844-682-1282

Illustrated by Stephen Armstrong

ISBN: 978-1-9822-7094-0 (sc)
ISBN: 978-1-9822-7095-7 (e)

Print information available on the last page.

Balboa Press rev. date: 08/04/2021

This is the story of three little fox children and how they learned to look for the good things that happen to them, and each of us, every day.

For good things, big or small, whether we notice it or not, happen daily to us all.

On a bitterly cold wintery night
when deep dark blackness took
over the light, and icy winds blew
the snow to left and to right...

A mother fox was worried... all her kits did was fight!

There was Jennie the oldest, and
Matty, the boy, and last but not
least, Manda, small... like a toy!

Not one of these
kits would say anything nice!
Their anger took over! Their
hearts were like ice!

So, Mom Fox did tell them,
"Make wrong into right!"

Then guess who showed up for a visit that night?

Well... Aunty Miz Foxy flew in on a flight!

She came from afar, a far away town.

But still, the children would not settle down!

While Mom went to run an errand
or two,

Foxy called to the kits, *"Yoo Hoo! Yoo Hoo!"*

She got their attention as sure as can be, and told them, *"Be quiet! Be quiet you three!"*

"I did not come here to listen to thee. Now, your mom was upset... don't you kits see?

Your yelling and fighting made her want to flee!

She works hard all day to feed all you three and when she needs rest, you won't let her be!

You might fight with each other but you'll not fight with me! I'm telling you kits, and you better well heed...

All of you sit there—no talking—don't blink!

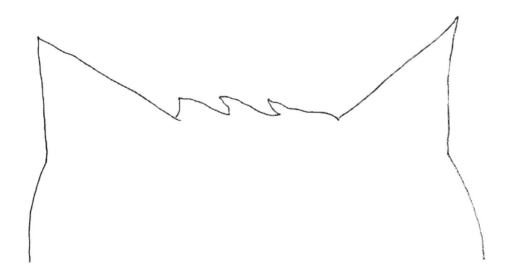

I want you to sit there.
Just sit there, and THINK!

*There must be one good thing
that happened today, and you
may not speak up 'til you've a
good thing to say!"*

So...
They sat.

And they sat...

Until Jennie then said,
*"Aunt Foxy!
A good thing popped into my
head!"*

"That's wonderful, Jennie,"
Aunt Foxy replied.
*"Please tell us about it and don't
you be shy!"*

So, she told them a story, a story
so swell...

...that it prompted boy Matty to share one as well!

Now here's where our story gets a little bit down.

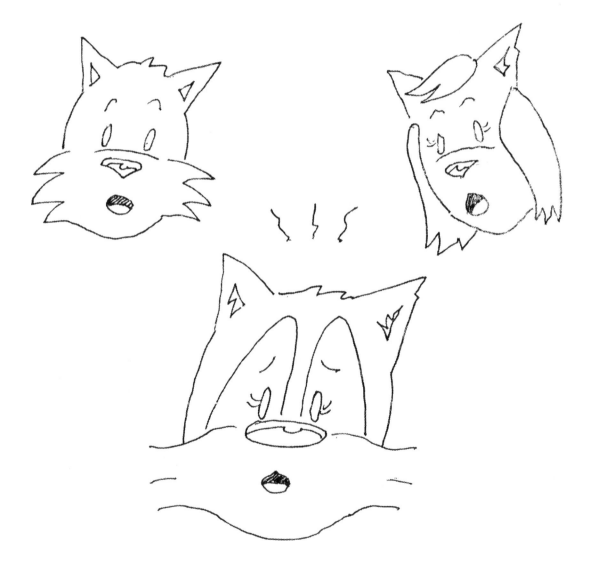

The others looked to li'l Manda,
and well...

...she just FROWNED!

As the two older children cajooled and cajoled...

...wise Aunt Miz Foxy
remembered, then told...

"My wee little niece, wipe that frown from your face. A good thing happened that has ribbons... and LACE!"

"You listen, and think... it was early today when I noticed your good thing and it happened this way..."

And that's when Miz Foxy
reminded the tot of her own
special thing that she had forgot!

"Your mom had to work... you wanted to play. In warm clothes she tried to dress you up for the day.

But you argued and fought 'til you got your own way...

*...and now you're wearing a dress
made to wear in warm May!*

And...

...your mom made that dress with her own magic hands!!

Isn't that special?
Isn't that grand?
So don't you be sad and don't
you be blue, because this was
the good thing that happened
to you!"

A smile slowly spread from each ear to ear.

Manda whispered, *"I wish Mom would hurry back here. I want to thank her, I very much should, for giving me this—my own something good!"*

A happy change overcame them
as Foxy knew that it would...
and so it went.

That one simple question turned all of their minds from the dreary details of everyday grinds.

It helped them to focus, no matter how small...

...on the good things that happen everyday to us ALL!

Now, tell me...

"What good thing happened to you today?"

Printed in the United States
by Baker & Taylor Publisher Services